FUN FACT FILE: US HISTORY!

20 FUN FACTS ABOUT THE DECLARATION OF INDEPENDENCE

By Heather Moore Niver

Gareth Stevens
Publishing

Please visit our website, www.garethstevens.com. For a free color catalog of all our high-quality books, call toll free 1-800-542-2595 or fax 1-877-542-2596.

Library of Congress Cataloging-in-Publication Data

Niver, Heather Moore.
20 fun facts about the Declaration of Independence / by Heather Moore Niver.
  p. cm. — (Fun fact file: US history)
Includes index.
ISBN 978-1-4339-9184-4 (pbk.)
ISBN 978-1-4339-9185-1 (6-pack)
ISBN 978-1-4339-9183-7 (library binding)
1. United States. Declaration of Independence—Juvenile literature. 2. United States—Politics and government—1775-1783—Juvenile literature. I. Niver, Heather Moore. II. Title.
E221.N58 2014
973.3'13—dc23

First Edition

Published in 2014 by
Gareth Stevens Publishing
111 East 14th Street, Suite 349
New York, NY 10003

Copyright © 2014 Gareth Stevens Publishing

Designer: Sarah Liddell
Editor: Greg Roza

Photo credits: Cover, p. 1 (declaration) Susan Law Cain/Shutterstock.com; cover, p.1 (painting) Victorian Traditions/Shutterstock.com; p. 5 English School/ The Bridgeman Art Library/Getty Images; pp. 6, 23 Stock Montage/Contributor/Archive Photos/Getty Images; p. 7 Interim Archives/Contributor/Archive Photos/Getty Images; p. 8 Hulton Archive/Stringer/Archive Photos/Getty Images; p. 9 Scott Rothstein/ Shutterstock.com; p. 10 EducationImages/UIG/Contributor/Universal Images Group/Getty Images; p. 11 photo courtesy of Wikimedia Commons, USA declaration independence.jpg; p. 12 photo courtesy of National Archives, declaration back.jpg; pp. 13, 14, 16 SuperStock/ SuperStock/Getty Images; p. 15 Todd Taulman/Shutterstock.com; p. 17 Photo Researchers/ Photo Researchers/Getty Images; p. 18 © iStockphoto.com/duncan1890; p. 19 (Franklin) Joseph Wright of Derby/The Bridgeman Art Library/Getty Images; pp. 19 (Rutledge), 20, 26–27 UniversalImagesGroup/Contributor/Universal Images Group/Getty Images; p. 21 photo courtesy of Wikimedia Commons, Johannes Adam Simon Oertel Pulling Down the Statue of King George III, N.Y.C ca. 1859.jpg; p. 22 photo courtesy of Wikimeda Commons, Lewis Morris painting.jpg; p. 24 Frank Scherschel/Contributor/Time & Life Pictures/Getty Images; p. 25 Tom Williams/Contributor/CQ-Roll Call Group/Getty Images; p. 29 © iStockphoto.com/smartstock.

Printed in the United States of America

CPSIA compliance information: Batch #CS13GS: For further information contact Gareth Stevens, New York, New York at 1-800-542-2595.

Contents

Words in the glossary appear in **bold** type the first time they are used in the text.

Fighting for Freedom

In 1620, about 100 British citizens sailed across the Atlantic Ocean. These early colonists and those who came after worked hard to **survive** in America but still had to pay taxes to Britain. Colonists didn't even have a say in the taxes passed by the British government, which became known as "taxation without **representation**."

Many colonists wanted independence from Great Britain, but King George III wouldn't agree. They wrote the Declaration of Independence, a **document** that announced their freedom to the world. It described **democratic** beliefs that are still important today.

The Declaration of Independence was signed in 1776, but the Revolutionary War didn't end until 1783.

FACT 1

At first, not all colonists liked the idea of independence.

In 1775, as the Revolutionary War started, few colonists thought they should be completely free from Britain. Those who wanted independence, like John Adams, were called "**radicals**." When Britain sent huge armies to the colonies, more and more colonists changed their minds and joined the radicals.

John Adams

Families of the signers were in danger, too. Francis Lewis's wife was put in prison and died from her treatment there.

The signers of the Declaration were in danger of being arrested...and sometimes worse.

King George didn't want the colonies to split from England. Members of the **Continental Congress** were called **traitors**. The king wanted to arrest them. Signing the Declaration of Independence was dangerous business. Signers risked losing their money, being put in jail, and even death.

Richard Stockton was put in prison and starved after signing the Declaration.

Four months after Richard Stockton signed the Declaration of Independence, the British threw him in jail. George Washington spoke out against the "the shocking . . . treatment" of Stockton. Richard almost died before he was freed.

Richard Stockton was able to get his family to safety before he was captured, but the British ruined his home.

FACT 4

The original Declaration of Independence is written on animal skin.

The first copy of the Declaration of Independence is written on a material called parchment. Parchment is made from animal skin that's treated with **lime** and stretched out. It lasts a long time. The original Declaration was probably either written on deerskin or calfskin.

The Declaration of Independence is written on parchment that is 24.25 by 29.75 inches (about 61.5 by 75.5 cm).

Copies of the Declaration of Independence were printed on July 4, 1776.

Copies of the Declaration of Independence were printed on paper. John Dunlap probably made more than 25 copies, called "Dunlap Broadsides." Copies were carried to towns and cities to be read aloud. One copy belonged to George Washington, the first US president.

George Washington

There is a handprint on the Declaration of Independence.

There is a handprint on the bottom left-hand corner of the Declaration of Independence. No one knows how it got there. The Declaration of Independence is so old that the handprint can't be cleaned off without damaging the parchment.

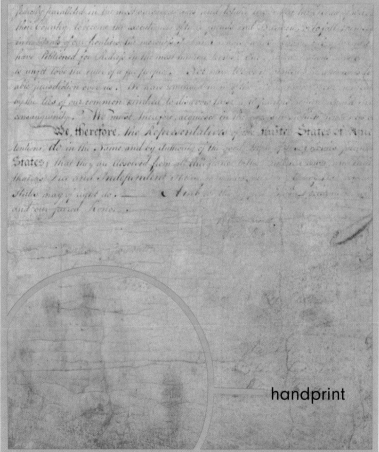

handprint

FACT 7

The writing on the back of the Declaration of Independence is upside down.

If you flip the original signed Declaration of Independence over and turn it upside down, you'll see writing. The very bottom line reads, "Original Declaration of Independence, dated 4th July 1776." No one knows who wrote it.

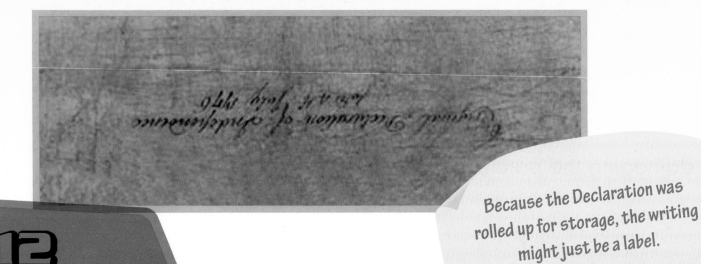

Because the Declaration was rolled up for storage, the writing might just be a label.

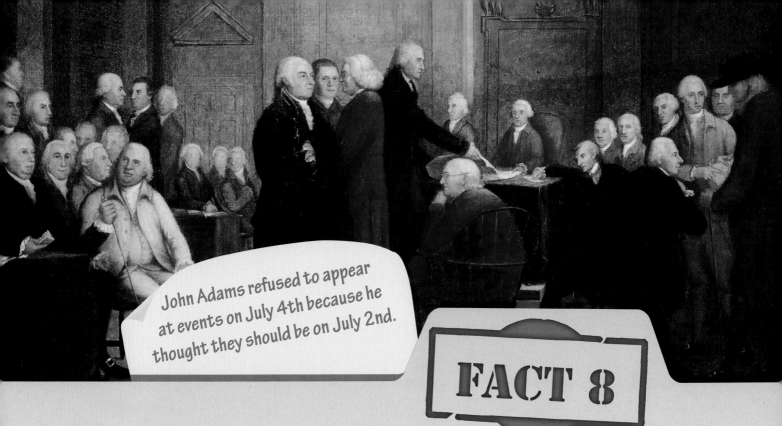

John Adams refused to appear at events on July 4th because he thought they should be on July 2nd.

The Continental Congress almost forgot to celebrate the first Independence Day.

The Continental Congress voted for the Declaration on July 2, 1776. It was approved on July 4, but no one signed it until August 2. The next year, no one thought to celebrate the vote until it was too late. Instead, they celebrated on July 4, 1777.

Writing the Declaration of Independence

Thomas Jefferson didn't want to write the Declaration.

Jefferson was only 33 years old in 1776 and one of the youngest members of Congress. He wasn't a lively speaker, but he was a great writer. He wanted John Adams to write the Declaration instead. Adams reportedly said, "You can write 10 times better than I can."

Thomas Jefferson

FACT 10

Flies annoyed Thomas Jefferson while he was writing the Declaration of Independence.

Thomas Jefferson went to a house in the country so he could concentrate on writing the Declaration. He stayed just outside the city of Philadelphia, Pennsylvania. As he wrote, he complained about the flies from the horse stable across the road.

At first, many people did not know that Thomas Jefferson wrote the Declaration.

It was many years before most Americans knew who wrote the Declaration of Independence. For almost 14 years, many Americans thought that the Continental Congress had written it. It wasn't until 1790 that people realized Jefferson was the author.

Thomas Jefferson wrote the main document, but Adams, Sherman, Franklin, and Livingston worked together to plan and later edit it.

FACT 12

Five writers worked on the Declaration of Independence.

Thomas Jefferson was not the only writer who worked on the Declaration. A group called the Committee of Five included John Adams, Roger Sherman, Benjamin Franklin, Robert Livingston, and Jefferson. They wrote a statement that explained to the world why the colonies wanted independence.

FACT 13

John Hancock has the biggest, longest signature on the Declaration.

With 56 names signed on the Declaration, you might think it would be hard to find the name of a certain **delegate**. Not if you're looking for John Hancock's name. His name is the largest. He was the first person to sign it, too.

Edward Rutledge

Benjamin Franklin

There's a 44-year age difference between the youngest and oldest signers of the Declaration.

The youngest person to sign the Declaration of Independence was only 26 years old. This was Edward Rutledge, who was a lawyer from South Carolina. The oldest signer was Benjamin Franklin. He was 70 years old when he signed.

FACT 15

Not one of the signers attended the first public reading of the Declaration.

The first time the Declaration of Independence was officially read aloud in public was on July 8, 1776. It was read in Philadelphia, Pennsylvania. None of the signers attended that reading.

FACT 16

When crowds in New York City heard a reading of the Declaration of Independence, they pushed over a statue.

It was July 9, 1776, when the news of the Declaration reached New York City. George Washington read it aloud in front of City Hall. The crowds were so excited that they pushed over a statue of King George III! The statue was melted down to make **ammunition** called musket balls.

21

FACT 17

New York was the only colony that didn't vote for the Declaration of Independence on July 4, 1776.

On July 4, 1776, only 12 of the 13 colonies voted for the Declaration of Independence. New York's delegates couldn't vote until their colony's government gave them permission. They didn't officially vote in favor of the Declaration until July 9, 1776.

When Lewis Morris— a delegate from New York— was warned that signing the Declaration was dangerous, he said, "Give me the pen."

Not everyone who voted for the Declaration put pen to parchment.

Robert Livingston was one of the Committee of Five, but he had to return to New York before he could sign. John Dickinson and Thomas Willing, both from Pennsylvania, didn't sign because they didn't think the colonies were prepared for war.

Before he worked on the Declaration, Robert Livingston was a member of the Continental Congress.

FACT 19

The Declaration of Independence was hidden underground during World War II.

During World War II, the Declaration was placed in a locked box that was sealed with lead and then placed in another, bigger box. All that protection weighed 150 pounds. Armed guards took it to Fort Knox in December 1941.

Fort Knox

The Declaration of Independence stayed at Fort Knox in Louisville, Kentucky, until 1944.

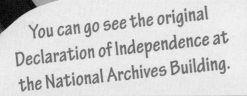
You can go see the original Declaration of Independence at the National Archives Building.

FACT 20

The Declaration is always protected by guards.

Today, the Declaration of Independence is stored at the National Archives Building in Washington, DC. Guards protect it all the time. It's stored in a case made of bulletproof glass and plastic. At night, it's kept in a special underground **vault**.

Declaration of Independence Timeline

Preparing the Declaration wasn't quick and easy. It took a lot of hard work, a lot of talk, and a lot of arguing. This timeline shows the steps the Continental Congress took as they crafted the Declaration of Independence.

1776

June 7
Congress is urged to declare independence from Great Britain.

June 11
The Committee of Five is chosen to write a declaration of independence.

June 12–27
Jefferson writes a declaration, and the committee reviews it.

June 28
A copy of the declaration is read in Congress.

July 1–4
Congress discusses and changes the declaration.

July 6
Pennsylvania *Evening Post* prints the first newspaper copies of the Declaration.

July 9
George Washington reads the Declaration in New York City. Delegates from New York officially vote in favor of the Declaration.

July 19
Congress orders an official copy of the Declaration to be made and signed by members.

1781
Thomas McKean, a delegate from Delaware, is the last person to sign the Declaration of Independence.

July 4
Congress accepts the Declaration of Independence.

July 8
The Declaration is first read in public in Philadelphia.

August 2
Delegates begin to sign the Declaration of Independence.

Groundbreaking Model

The Declaration of Independence was the first official document that announced a nation's independence. Other countries have modeled their own governments after it. France used it during the French Revolution (1787–1799).

The Declaration of Independence is one of the most important documents in American history. It explains why the colonies should be independent. The Declaration also talks about how a government can be run to be fair to everyone. No wonder this "letter to George" is one of the greatest political documents ever written.

In CONGRESS, JULY 4, 1776.

unanimous Declaration of the thirteen united States of America,

Glossary

ammunition: bullets, shells, and other things fired by weapons

Continental Congress: the government of the 13 colonies

delegate: a representative of one of the 13 colonies

democratic: treating everyone as equals

document: a formal piece of writing

lime: a powder made from limestone or seashells that is used for many purposes, including making parchment

radical: a person with views very different from the usual, especially related to politics

representation: the act of standing for a group of people

survive: to live through something

traitor: someone who goes against their government

vault: an underground safe

For More Information

Books

Leavitt, Amie J. *The Declaration of Independence in Translation: What It Really Means.* Mankato, MN: Capstone Press, 2008.

Osornio, Catherine L. *The Declaration of Independence from A to Z.* Gretna, LA: Pelican, 2010.

Websites

The Declaration of Independence
www.archives.gov/exhibits/charters/declaration_join_the_signers.html
Learn more about who signed the Declaration, check out a Declaration timeline, and even sign it yourself!

The Declaration of Independence
www.ushistory.org/declaration/
Learn more about the Declaration of Independence with information about the signers, timelines, and other related events.

Index